Sports Concussions and Getting Back in the Game... of Life

Sports Concussions and Getting Back in the Game... of Life

A SOLUTION FOR CONCUSSION SYMPTOMS INCLUDING HEADACHES, LIGHT SENSITIVITY, POOR ACADEMIC PERFORMANCE, ANXIETY AND OTHERS... THE IRLEN METHOD

Helen Irlen

ISBN: 1522889566
ISBN 13: 9781522889564

Table of Contents

Introduction

My reason for writing this book is my dedication to helping those with sports and combat-related concussions as well as more serious head injuries. In just the past three years, I have seen close to 300 youths and adults with post-concussive syndrome for whom the Irlen Method has been a life saver. It is a fact that both youth and professional athletes don't always report their injuries and end up back in the game too soon. It is important to build a safer environment for everyone involved in sports in order to prevent concussions. However, that alone is not enough. Playing it safe can't be the only answer. Athletes also need to understand the importance of reporting their injuries when they occur. As hard as we try to protect athletes from such injuries through new rules, better equipment, proper teaching of the fundamentals and a greater awareness of the issue, injuries will still occur. Sports are such a major aspect of society and one in which concussions are part of the package. Unfortunately, the symptoms of concussions and head injuries are far more widespread than most of us realize. For that reason, teammates, coaches, and parents also need be able to recognize the signs, symptoms, and need for proper treatment of concussions when they believe that one may have occurred. Education is important. Be informed and be safe.

Just as we encourage everyone to drive safely and wear seat belts at all times, accidents on the roads will still occur. Some will be minor fender benders and others far more serious. The same holds true in sports. Many injuries will be minor bumps, bruises, cuts, and sprains. However, even wearing helmets, taking other precautions, and playing by the rules cannot stop concussions and head injuries from occurring.

Hopefully, they will occur less often; but they are still a possibility, whether you're playing in a stadium in front of 50,000 spectators or on a local field with a bunch of friends.

In this book we will talk about the modern culture of sports and why there is an escalating number of concussions. We also define a concussion as well as post-concussion syndrome. We will discuss the need for children and parents to be diligent and look for symptoms, and we will talk about what doctors can and can't do. We will encourage children to speak up and parents to listen. We will include some precautions and then take a look at the long-term picture and what happens when concussion symptoms do not go away within seven to ten days, or weeks, or months, or even years.

And, finally, what this book also features, that other books on the subject do not, is information on a remarkable technique for restoring brain functioning so that the individual is able to lead a normal productive life after a concussion. The Irlen Method has earned millions of fans by providing a long-term, well-documented, and scientifically-proven solution that directly addresses many of the signs and symptoms of post-concussive syndrome. Backed by over 30 years of research, Irlen is the pioneer and global leader in the visual processing technology that has helped millions of adults and children around the world.

It is my hope that you will share this important information with others so that we can save lives, restore lives, and get people back in the game...of life.

CHAPTER 1

The New Founded Awareness of Concussions in Sports

*D*id you know that roughly every 21 seconds, someone in the United States has a concussion or another type of serious brain injury? And one of the most common reasons people get concussions and head injuries is through playing sports.
This is America; and we are a country, not unlike many others, that is obsessed with sports. We play sports, watch sports, talk about the games, and perhaps even bet on them. There are 24/7 sports radio and television channels, billions of dollars of sports apparel sold every year, and sports bars from coast to coast. Yes, we love our sports.

Sports can be a huge part of life; and for millions of young athletes, it is just that. We encourage our children to get into sports at an early age. This can be very constructive since there are many positives about being involved in athletics, including the benefits of physical exercise, the fresh air, the camaraderie of team activities, the skills learned, coordination building, and the sportsmanship that comes from participating in sports. In many instances, sports can also build confidence and increase self-esteem. Parents, educators, and trainers also point out that participating in sports helps children:

- Build character
- Learn to set goals
- Learn to work together to accomplish a goal
- Discover personal strengths, skills, and weaknesses
- Interact with people from various cultural backgrounds

And playing sports can be fun, fulfilling and, if you're extremely proficient, financially rewarding. For many youngsters, athletics can open the door to college scholarships and lifetime friendships.

There is, however, the other side of sports; the darker side...injuries. One type of injury that has generated a lot of attention of late is concussions. There has been a steady increase in the number of youngsters suffering concussions from sports. Either that, or concussions are finally being taken seriously and being reported. It is estimated that there are over 1.6 million sports-related concussions in the United States each year, of which between 136,000 and 300,000 are sustained by high school students.

These numbers do not include the youngsters who told their coaches, their parents, and everyone else that they were fine while their head was throbbing. They may very well have had concussions but did not share the information for fear of not being allowed to play. Yes, there are more concussions, and other head injuries, then those that are reported to coaches, parents, medical trainers, or doctors. In fact, an ESPN poll indicated that 33 percent of college football players have lied about concussions.

The minimizing of concussions in sports has now become a major health priority. At least once a week, if not more, we are reminded by TV reports, newspaper articles, or websites reporting that sports-related concussions are a very real problem. Articles have appeared in the *New York Times, Los Angeles Times, Washington Post, U.S News and World Report, the Huffington Post*, and on WebMD.com, mayoclinic.org, MedlinePlus.com, and numerous other media outlets. Dr. Neil Alpiner, a pediatric concussion specialist in Royal Oaks, Michigan, even has an ongoing concussion blog. The *Wall Street Journal*, not long ago, featured a story about the fact that many youngsters are returning to sports too soon without having sufficient time to rest or recover after a concussion or blow to the head. This has also been an important concern of many parents and has been addressed in many articles and news reports – children who keep on playing when they should be taking care of their brain.

In May of 2012, the NBC news program *Rock City* aired a special report on teenage girls playing soccer in Chester Hills, Pennsylvania. Like so many teens around the country, they played the game in a league environment and loved the camaraderie and the competition. The particular teens featured in the segment had become pretty good players as well. However, the sport they had grown to love proved costly, affecting them in ways they never imagined.

After five concussions, one of the teenagers featured on the program, Allison, described herself to *Rock Center* reporter Kate Snow by saying that she should wear a sign telling people "my head is broken." The 15-year-old was only able to attend school for four hours a day. She had to sleep in a room with soft blue lights and ate dinner with her family by candlelight. Headaches and extreme light sensitivity had become the norm for Allison, who, along with several other girls on her team and thousands of others around the country, was struggling with the after-effects of concussions. One of Allison's friends had her first concussion from playing soccer at the age of 12 and by 14 was also struggling with symptoms that were similar to those of Allison. Neither girl could lead the "normal" life of a teenager.

Sure, we are told that concussions typically go away in a few days or may last up to three weeks. That is the normal perception...concussions will simply disappear. But what if they last longer or never fully disappear? As Allison and others can attest to, longer lasting symptoms can occur and can change the life of a youngster or an adult. This book will present a solution for these residual problems.

We've had athletes like Nick Bell, a former running back in the NFL, as well as NHL hockey players among others, come to the Irlen Institute looking for help. Bell came more than 15 years after the end of his NFL career that had left him with a lifetime of disabilities. Of course, it's not only athletes who get concussions. In recent years, we've also been working with many of our brave men and women of the military who have sustained head injuries and concussions. Like the athletes, they come to us looking for help. Irlen Spectral Filters can provide significant help with the symptoms associated with head injuries, alleviating them or making them go away completely.

CHAPTER 2

Silence and the Modern Day Culture of Sports

Why don't your kids tell you when they have a headache, blurred vision, dizziness, nausea, or other signs of a concussion?

Why don't children want you to know?

Athletes, especially young ones, don't want to let anyone down. Sports were once played by youngsters primarily for fun. Kids made the rules, played the games, and had nobody else to answer to. For the most part, those days are gone. Competitive sports for children have taken on an entirely new culture of their own. The increase in head injuries in recent years is not puzzling to anyone aware of the significant emphasis placed on performance and on the importance of playing harder. In order to keep their coaching jobs, or simply for their own egos, coaches are pushing children harder than ever.

Hitting harder, being aggressive, and winning have been elevated to the new mantra. Kids must do whatever it takes to make the team and then keep their spot in the starting lineup (which also prompted the steroid problem in sports as well) and that means playing harder no matter how they feel. Unfortunately, while more and more athletes are flocking onto the fields to play, many youngsters are not skilled in how to properly tackle in football, how to check in hockey, the right way to head a ball in soccer, or how to perform in other sports in a way in which they may avoid injuries. In addition to needing the necessary skills, the developing bodies, including the brains, of young athletes are more susceptible to injuries than those of adults. For example, a soccer ball traveling 30 yards and landing on the head of a young girl of 12 or 15 years of age, with still developing neck muscles, can be far more damaging than if it was landing on the head of a more physically mature woman. This explains why there has been a significant increase in concussions in girls' soccer.

In fact, studies now show that girls who play soccer in middle school have high rates of concussions. Researchers watched 351 girls playing soccer over an extended period of time and saw that 59 of the girls got concussions, which is more than 15%, a higher percentage than other sports concussion rates. Sadly, only about 50% sought medical attention while nearly 60% continued to play.

When you combine the following factors:

- More youngsters getting involved in organized sports
- Coaches pushing children harder than ever before
- Young teens' desire to excel at any cost
- The developing biological makeup of young athletes and
- The, often, underdeveloped skill sets...

...you have greater potential for injuries. As a result, we are seeing this increase in the number of concussions and other head injuries.

But it's not only the coaches by any means. Sports today are big money. Professional athletes make a fortune. We once wanted out children to grow up to be doctors or lawyers. Today, a professional athlete is higher on the wish list. Many parents push children harder than ever to excel in sports, even more so than they push them academically. One very significant reason is that scholarship money can pay for the spiraling costs of higher education, and a top athlete is more likely to get a free ride than a top student.

Whether it's an ego thing, a means of living vicariously through their child's success or going for that college scholarship, many parents are pushing their children harder than ever before. "It's called the Little League Parent Syndrome," says Dr. Andrew Yellen, a California-based licensed psychologist specializing in both clinical and sports psychology. Yellen also played college football and then spent many years coaching at the high-school level. He sees how the obnoxious little league parent of old has taken on a whole new meaning today.

"My son, who is a football coach for the University of Houston, almost got into blows with the irate father of one of the team's star players because he would not let the player into the game following a head injury and possible concussion," says Yellen. That mentality is pervasive in a lot of places. "When I coached, every year I would sit down with the parents and tell them that the fastest way your son can get benched on my team is for me to find out that he had an injury and didn't tell me. I didn't care how insignificant; I'm even talking about a blister. I made it clear that if their son had an injury and did not come to me with that injury, he would be benched. I was very adamant about it – I wanted to be the one to make the decision as a trained professional. But not everyone operates that way," explains Yellen.

With unyielding pressure coming from coaches and parents, is it any wonder why your child is not going to tell you that he or she is dizzy, tired, or having headaches for days or even weeks? Kids do not want to lose their place on the roster or their image as an athlete, which rates very high at all levels of sports. Youngsters look up to athletes and buy into their incredible stardom. They have been doing so for years. Today, however, athletes have become the new rock stars with what appears to be the ideal life – playing a game they love, making a fortune, and being adored by millions. Why would you jeopardize becoming a star athlete by letting it be known that you are in pain? Nick Bell, former NFL running back, noted that back in the 1990s, the college coaches did not want to hear if something was bothering you, especially headaches or dizziness. "Essentially, if you complained, you didn't play and that would end your chance at becoming a pro. So you shut up about it. There is simply too much at stake for many youngsters to speak up about their symptoms," says Bell.

Sadly, in many cases, there is also too much at stake for many parents to listen to their kids when they do speak up. The combination of a struggling economy and very high college tuitions has had an impact upon the health and welfare of teenagers whose families see sports scholarships as a ticket to a better life...but at what cost?

The movie *Varsity Blues*, from back in 1999, brought the issue to the surface when an egocentric football coach in a small Texas town, who worshiped high school football, put his players in physical danger for his own ego. To make it worse, the parents supported the coach as they saw football and scholarships to college as the only way out of their small town. The film, ahead of its time, is very apropos to today's sports culture, especially in many small economically-challenged communities.

CHAPTER 3

It's Not Only Football Players

It's not just the competitive "athletes" in football, soccer, or team sports that are sustaining head and neck injuries. Skiing, skateboarding, ice skating, and martial arts are only a few of the many sports in which athletes can also experience a concussion or head injury. Whether you consider cheerleading a sport or an activity, there is also a rise in the number of head injuries amongst cheerleaders.

While watching cheerleaders on the sidelines or in competitions, one typically does not see very many accidents or injuries. Routines are well-honed by the time they are performed on the sidelines of a game or at halftime on the field. However, numerous mishaps occur during practice where many parents, athletes, and coaches fail to recognize the potential injuries from pyramids and other stunts on the developing neck and back muscles. The female-dominated sport/activity comes complete with lifts and flying; and statistics show that 30,000 cheerleaders end up in emergency rooms every year, many from landing on their necks or heads while learning and practicing their routines.

An ABC News report on injuries from cheerleading focused attention on the problem and featured UCLA Spirit Squad Director, and former cheerleader, Molly Vehling who explained that the well-known college has a head cheer coach, an assistant cheer coach, a dance team coach, and a trainer. She also added that the school strictly adheres to the guidelines set up by the American Association of Cheerleading Coaches and Administrators (AACCA) which put limits on pyramid height, thrower-to-flier ratio, the number of spotters used, and so on. She also points out that cheerleaders need a certain level of physical fitness and training to do pyramids, stunting, or tumbling.

Unfortunately, because cheerleading is not recognized as a sport at most high schools or middle schools, it receives a very limited budget and is often run by an untrained volunteer. As a result, many schools fall far short on the level of safety precautions and instruction of a school such as UCLA.

Deanna, who works with us at the Irlen Institute in Southern California, provides the antithesis of the UCLA story. Her daughter, at age 13, was on a middle school cheerleading squad that was overseen by an English teacher and trained by a 13-year-old boy who created routines based on those his older sister did for a competitive cheerleading squad. The problem, as Deanna explained, was that he had no experience training anyone, much less teenage girls whose neck and back muscles are still developing. As she watched from the sidelines, Deanna noted that her daughter spoke up regularly and told the inexperienced trainer when they simply could not do something that he had concocted based on watching his sister's far-more-advanced squad. "I was ready to step in if necessary," added Deanna, also noting that when the cheerleading squad did a routine on talent night at the school, complete with lifts and flips, most of the parents in the audience gasped, unaware that these young cheerleaders were attempting such stunts with no real (or trained) supervision. Deanna, who wanted her daughter to make the decision, was relieved when her daughter and five other team members all quit, fearing for their safety in such an unsupervised setting ripe with the potential for injury.

The sad reality is that many schools around the country are in a similar situation to that of Deanna's daughter, with a squad headed by a teacher who got roped into the role of supervisor or was once a cheerleader years ago. As a result, cheerleading accounts for more than 67% of catastrophic injuries among high school female athletes, and middle schools' statistics can't be far behind.

The parents of the 500,000+ cheerleaders from middle school through college need to be proactive and, like Deanna, monitor what is going on. They need to make sure the school is accountable for the safety and well-being of their participants... this holds true for all physical activities.

"Just say no." Nancy Reagan popularized this saying as an anti-drug message. Teenagers also need to learn to be proactive and speak up if they are asked to do something that appears to be too physically demanding. This runs the gamut from sports to other physical activities. Far too many injuries occur when youngsters are pushed too hard and too far. Volunteer coaches, like the 13-year-old who is training a cheerleading squad or the "little league dads," have no idea of the physical abilities of the kids on their squads or teams. Many are also at a complete loss of what to do if and when an injury occurs. Therefore, the children and the parents need to be ready to speak up before injuries occur.

CHAPTER 4

All About Concussions and
Head Injuries

Before we continue the discussion of concussions and head injuries, we should:

1. Define a concussion
2. Review the signs and symptoms of a concussion
3. Discuss children / teens and concussions

Definition

The Mayo Clinic defines a concussion as: *A traumatic brain injury that alters the way your brain functions.*

To be more technical, the brain, which is made up of soft tissue and protected inside the skull by spinal fluid, gets jarred enough to move around and possibly even bang against the skull. Blood vessels can be torn, and nerves can be injured. Although concussions are most often caused by a blow to the head, they can occur when the head and upper body are violently shaken.

Symptoms

There are several resulting symptoms of a concussion including:

- Headaches
- Dizziness
- Lightheadedness
- Nausea and / or vomiting
- Light sensitivity
- Blurred vision
- Slurred speech
- Confusion
- Loss of some coordination
- Memory loss
- Tiredness
- Irritability
- Difficulty thinking or focusing
- A loss of consciousness

It is often believed that someone has to lose consciousness to have a concussion. That, however, is not true. Most often, people who get concussions remain conscious at all times. Loss of consciousness for more than a minute can mean a more complex, serious concussion.

Some, but not necessarily all, of the above symptoms can indicate a concussion. How long the symptoms last indicates the severity of that concussion. Most concussion symptoms subside within 7 to 10 days. In an effort to allow someone with a concussion to properly recover, it is advised that the individual rests the brain for at least that time period, meaning that they avoid sports and literally try not to think too hard. A second concussion, or multiple concussions, can be more serious, even if individually they do not appear to be serious or last very long. The cumulative effects of concussions can result in more prolonged symptoms and what is called post-concussion (or post-concussive) syndrome (PSC). In some cases, this can occur from one serious concussion. PSC will be discussed in more detail later.

Children and Teens

Research from the *American Journal of Sports Medicine* indicates that younger athletes may be at greater risk of damage from concussion because their brains are not fully developed.

It is the developing brain and neck muscles that can cause more severe damage in a younger person. Their heads are simply not as steady on their shoulders. Should a younger athlete take a big hit in a football game or be involved in a collision in soccer or hockey, the brain is more likely to move inside the skull, resulting in a concussion.

Research has also shown that young women may suffer more symptoms than young men because of higher estrogen levels. This may exacerbate brain injuries, as well as greater rates of blood flow and higher metabolic needs in the brain, which may make symptoms more pronounced. Females may also take longer to recover from a concussion than their male counterparts, particularly young women.

The findings suggest that because of anatomical differences that make them more vulnerable, female athletes, and younger athletes in particular, may need to be managed more cautiously after a concussion.

Associate professor of kinesiology at Michigan State University, Dr. Tracey Covassin, notes that "Parents need to understand that if their daughter has a concussion, she may potentially take longer to recover from that concussion than their son who is a football player."

Along with gender, age is also a factor in recovery. Studies by Dr. Covassin, of roughly 300 young athletes in four states who had sustained concussions, showed that high school athletes performed comparatively worse for their age than older college athletes on measures of verbal and visual memory. More symptoms were reported by the female athletes than the male athletes in the study. In addition, the cognitive impairments also lasted three times longer in the high school students than the college students.

While anyone who has a concussion should take the proper amount of time to recover, the American Academy of Pediatrics encourages a longer time frame for full recovery for children and adolescents, gender notwithstanding. They take a cautious stand regarding children returning to sports or school too soon, stating that:

Children with concussions usually make a complete recovery within three weeks, but you need to consult a specialist when the recovery takes longer than that. They're recommending that they should rest and make a slow transition back to school in order to allow the brain to heal. However, management of concussion cases should be individualized because every concussion is unique and encompasses a different constellation and severity of symptoms.

While doctors will run neurological tests, the symptoms, as reported by the injured person or as witnessed by people around the injured person, can help determine how severe the concussion really is. However, one of the problems of self-assessment, or those of other lay people, is accuracy. Since medical tests cannot determine if you have had a concussion or even the severity of a concussion, we find ourselves relying heavily on the reporting of the individual, which can be incomplete when that individual is an athlete looking to return to action or a coach who wants his or her athlete on the field sooner than later.

As a result, we are using certain standards that may not always indicate whether or not a child has received a concussion. In some cases, a child eager to play will downplay symptoms and a concussion will go undiagnosed, while the potentially serious consequences of ignoring a blow to the brain remain.

CHAPTER 5

Talking With Your Child About Concussions

Watching your son or daughter score a goal, a touchdown, a basket, spike a volleyball, or get a base hit are exhilarating moments that you can share. From soccer to lacrosse to wrestling, there are youngsters excelling at a wide range of athletic activities on school teams or in youth leagues all over the country. Supporting your child's love of the game is wonderful, and you can share the excitement and joy of such activities.

However, along with recounting the highs and lows in the sport, you also need to discuss the safety issues. Just as you would do before handing over the keys to the car, you also need to introduce safety issues into the context of sports. While you do not want to be preachy, you do want your child to understand that injuries do occur and that there is a need to take necessary precautions. It may be as simple as wearing a helmet when riding a bike (which reduces the risk of concussion by 85% and is a law in most communities) or always wearing a batting helmet before stepping into the batter's box in baseball – which is mandatory throughout all organized baseball programs, at every level. Padding, protective helmets, and other gear are part of sports; and most kids are well aware of that, even from watching their heroes on TV. Fortunately, helmets prevent numerous injuries in sports, just as seatbelts do in cars. Unfortunately, even with all of the precautions in place, accidents do happen; and parents and coaches should be responsible for making sure that your athletes take the necessary precautions.

As a parent, however, you need to go one step farther. You need to establish an open line of communications with your son or daughter. You want to let them know that it is vital that they tell you when something is wrong, just as Dr. Yellen did as a coach, insisting that he know about all injuries of any kind. Your child needs to be encouraged to tell you when something is wrong. Remind him or her that you love them and that as much as you want to see them succeed, you also want to know if there is any type of physical problem. Review with them the symptoms of a concussion and remind them that you do not have to lose consciousness to have one. There are numerous stories of people who have struggled with concussion symptoms, including some coming up later in this book, which you can share if you feel that such examples can help you get your point across.

Make sure they understand that rest is important if they have a concussion or any type of head injury. Remind them that returning to the game, or even to school, too soon can make concussion symptoms worse. While they may balk at not being able to play, they may be relieved at missing a few days or a few weeks of school. Teachers should also be aware that concussions are real and not an excuse to stay home from school. Support your argument for taking time off from sports by letting young athletes know that even professional sports leagues are now taking more precautions and not letting athletes back on the field if they do not feel they are ready to return. The National Football League makes players leave a game if there is a sign of a concussion, and they are checked out during the ensuing week before returning. Major League Baseball has a new 7 Day Disabled List for players with concussions. The point is that since youngsters look at the pros as role models, they can see that they, too, are being mindful if they have a concussion and are not returning to action too soon.

Also explain that multiple head injuries are a serious matter, even if they are not all considered concussions. The label "concussion" is not as important as the effects of repeated blows to the head. Parents and coaches owe it to young athletes to clearly discuss the potential for concussions and the need for honest communications / transparency—you need to know if any of your athletes has such symptoms. Make a deal with them, offer something your son or daughter enjoys, from a video game to a dinner out at their favorite restaurant after the season, if they promise to be forthright and tell you about any and all injuries or physical discomfort during the season. It's a worthwhile trade off.

Symptom Awareness is Vital

After a serious blow to the head in any sport, at any level, the idea of a possible concussion is finally becoming an immediate reaction. Broadcasters are commenting as soon as a player is slow to get up, and alert parents and coaches are also gaining concussion symptom awareness. This is encouraging. It shows that the media is reaching more people and spreading the word about the seriousness of the situation. There are, however, still many more coaches and parents who need to be able to distance themselves from the outcome of the game (or their son or daughter's potential scholarship) and be aware of the signs of a concussion during a game as well as afterwards.

A child may appear to be back to normal, getting back in action, but there may be immediate signs the something is not right. He or she may:

- Appear dazed or stunned
- Seem unbalanced or move clumsily
- Be slow to react
- Have slower hand-eye coordination
- Forget upcoming plays or instructions
- Not remember the score
- Keep holding their head or looking down
- Exhibit behavioral changes during the game: for example, he or she may be less aggressive than usual and may even appear tentative or frightened to participate in the action

Yes, there are ways to tell if an athlete, young or older, does not appear to be himself or herself out there on the field, the court, or anywhere the activity is taking place. Coaches and parents should be tuned in.

You can also see symptoms in ensuing days, such as the following. He or she may:

- Still be having headaches
- Experience behavioral changes
- Have trouble with school or other activities
- Have blurry vision
- Experience balance or coordination problems
- Have memory difficulties

- Have difficulty remembering and retaining new information
- Be sensitive to light or noise
- Be more moody than usual
- Have difficulty concentrating on school work
- Have difficulty paying attention in class
- Need additional time to complete school assignments
- Get easily upset
- Be more emotional than usual
- Have difficulty going to sleep or staying asleep
- Be sleeping more than usual

It's important to be aware of what to look for once a child has had any type of head injury to make a fair determination of whether the symptoms have indeed disappeared, or not. This also means asking questions in a caring manner. After all, kids don't like to answer questions if they feel you are giving them the third degree.

While you may not ask all of the questions at once, you want to find out how they are feeling and if they have physical symptoms. Ask questions such as:

- Are you getting tired while you're in school?
- Have you been feeling dizzy or nauseous?
- Do you have frequent or infrequent headaches during the day?
- Do you have frequent or ongoing stomachaches?
- Is school work harder than it used to be?
- Are you light sensitive?
- Does sun light or the fluorescent lighting at school bother you?

Explain to children and teens the importance of being honest when it comes to injuries. Remember that the prolonged symptoms from head injuries can even affect their ability to go to college and have a career. Also, keep in mind as you are reading that the symptoms mentioned above and throughout this book, which do not disappear with rest and time, can be addressed and resolved with precision Irlen Spectral Filters, which will be discussed later on in this book.

Note: An article from *U.S.A. Today* stated that students should take a slower path, not only back to sports but to increased mental activity. While this may not sit well with instructors, it may be worthwhile to have a doctor back you up in advocating for your child's health. The article cited a study that indicated: *Among 335 8- to 23-year-olds who suffered a concussion, those with the highest level of cognitive activity after the injury took about 100 days on average to completely recover, compared with about 20 to 50 days for less mentally active peers, researchers found. The findings, published in the Journal of Pediatrics, support the benefits of cognitive rest following a concussion.*

CHAPTER 6

Post-Concussion Syndrome

Post-Concussion Syndrome, as defined by the Mayo Clinic, is: *A complex disorder in which a variable combination of post-concussion symptoms — such as headaches and dizziness — that last for weeks and sometimes months after the injury that caused the concussion. In most people, post-concussion syndrome symptoms occur within the first seven to ten days and go away within three months, though they can persist for a year or more.*

They also add: *The risk of post-concussion syndrome doesn't appear to be associated with the severity of the initial injury.*

Beth Israel Deaconess Medical Center, in Boston, Massachusetts, notes that: *As time passes, the relationship of symptom severity and the medical measures of brain injury becomes less certain. Many of the problems caused by the injury appear to persist, even when brain recovery has taken place. Individuals who continue to report symptoms months after their injuries also commonly report emotional distress and poor physical functioning. The persistence of symptoms similar to the acute symptoms of concussion is called the post-concussion syndrome (PCS).*

They also categorize the symptoms of post-concussive syndrome (PCS) into three categories: somatic (physical), cognitive (brain function), and emotional (psychological). Again, while they emphasize that most PCS symptoms will disappear within three to six months, this is not the case for all people. For those who have had repeated injuries to the head, this can take longer.

Unfortunately, we have seen these symptoms last for many years. The problem is that while there are some means of measuring concussions, there is no clear understanding of how and why such symptoms persist over time for certain people and not others. Dr. Yellen points to former athletes, some of whom are managing very well after repeated blows to the head in contact sports, while others are struggling at simple tasks 10 or even 20 years after playing.

The most common symptoms of post-concussive syndrome, as categorized by the Beth Israel Deaconess Medical Center, are:

Physical (somatic) symptoms
Headaches
Dizziness
Nausea and motion sickness
Photosensitivity
Insomnia and fatigue

Cognitive symptoms
Poor concentration and action lapses
Memory problems, poor recall, and mental fatigue
Feel like in a "fog"
Easily confused

Emotional (psychological) symptoms
Anxiety
Depression
Irritability – this is not a direct symptom of a brain injury but may occur as a result of the frustration and anxiety emanating from other symptoms.

It is very important that you remain conscientious when it comes to following up a head injury, even if it is not classified as a "concussion." Watch your child over time and be aware of anything unusual, such as a sudden drop in academic performance, as noted earlier. Continue to ask some questions when you can and remind them that it is simply out of love and concern.

If you see, while tracking your child's behaviors and academic performance, that he or she has performed poorly for several days or weeks after a concussion but then resumed more typical levels in their activities, then it is likely that the symptoms from the concussion have subsided. However, if you see patterns developing over the long term, you may be dealing with post-concussion syndrome.

CHAPTER 7

What Can Doctors Do?

I f you think you have a concussion, you want to see a doctor – and this is not just advice for a youngster, but for anyone, regardless of whether it is the result of playing sports or any type of accidental blow to the head.

Unlike a bruise or even a broken wrist or arm, there is nothing a doctor can immediately do to treat a concussion. Much of the diagnosis is built around the visible symptoms, such as vomiting, and answers to the questions regarding symptoms and the injury itself. A doctor will discuss your symptoms (including all of those listed above) and ask questions to determine how well the brain is functioning. This can include a neurological exam which consists of checking vision, hearing, coordination/ motor skills, speech, and balance as well as asking questions to test your memory and ability to concentrate.

A doctor will also want to know about your work or sports history and any recent injuries, especially blows to the head or previous concussions. The severity of a concussion is hard to diagnose on its own. The number of symptoms, or whether or not someone loses consciousness, does not measure severity. Previous concussions, time of recovery, age, and how recently there were other blows to the head, or other concussions, will be more significant factors in the potential severity of the injury. For this reason, a doctor will want to monitor the concussion process to recovery.

In most cases, a doctor will send someone with a concussion home to rest and advise that person not to participate in sports or any extra-curricular activities for a week. Right after the concussion, the doctor will want someone to stay with the individual and try not to let them fall asleep. If, however, the person is able to hold a conversation and is not showing other symptoms, such as dilated pupils or issues with walking, the doctor will usually tell them they can sleep. Let your doctor give you his or her specific advice regarding sleep.

When dealing with younger children, parents are typically advised to wake the child up a few times during the night to see how he or she is feeling.

It's important to understand that head injuries may not show up in medical tests. However, that does not mean the patient is not suffering with headaches, fatigue, anxiety, or sleep problems. For this reason, much of your diagnosis depends on what you say and how good your doctor is at listening. Some doctors swear by tests and assume that anything not showing up in brain scans is "just stress" or perhaps something else that shall simply pass. Other doctors take greater interest in what you tell them and recognize that sometimes symptoms may not show up in their tests. If you have persisting problems and your doctor isn't responding beyond looking at test results, find another doctor who understands head injuries and listens to you.

Brain Scans

As a precaution or to better assess a brain or head injury, a doctor may recommend a CT scan or MRI, especially for a younger patient or someone who has had at least one previous concussion. This can show if there is subarachnoid hemorrhaging (bleeding in the brain), if there is a brain tumor, or other types of significant abnormalities.

- **CT Scan** - a computerized x-ray that provides images of the brain (or other parts of the body) so that it can be seen on a monitor. They can usually show swelling or bleeding from the brain.
- **MRI Scan** (Magnetic Resonance Imaging test) - provides detailed pictures of the brain using magnetic energy instead of radiation
- **SPECT Scan** (Single Photon Emission Computed Tomography) - imaging is a functional scan which allows you to see blood flow in the brain and provide a better functional analysis.
- **PET Scans** (Positron Emission Tomography) and SPECT Scans are similar types of functional brain scans. This is a nuclear medical imaging technique that produces a three-dimensional image or picture of functional processes

in the brain. It has become an often used functional brain scan prescribed by many neurologists to get an understanding of the brain functioning and be better able to treat patients.

Unfortunately, concussion symptoms do not always appear immediately, may be subtle at first, and often cannot be diagnosed by a CT or MRI brain scan.

CHAPTER 8

Baseline and Sideline Tests

J ust by observing, you can gain some insight into what is going on with your child. Start with a baseline, if possible, which is essentially a list of a person's behaviors prior to the injury. This can include how they did in school academically as well as how they acted or reacted in other situations. Did bright light bother them in the past? Have you seen a change in coordination or motor skills? Were they easily frustrated? Knowing their previous behavioral patterns and comparing them to their current behaviors can allow you to make comparisons and determine whether or not you see ongoing behavioral changes. Next, you'll want to track their behaviors and academic performance over the ensuing weeks and months.

You are looking for indicators that there is still something wrong. Remember, a child may not come forth and tell you. What often happens is that the child becomes so used to the headache or light sensitivity that he or she begins to think it is normal to be living with these problems. Therefore, they stop reporting them. A drop in academic performance also may not be reported since your child does not want to disappoint you.

While some children can track their own behavior, most often it will fall on your shoulders as a parent to use what you observe in conjunction with simple questions and observations to determine how far he or she has moved away from his/her baseline behaviors. Some children may have been sensitive to bright lighting prior to the head injury, so you will have to ask if he or she is feeling more sensitive. Other students were not doing particularly well in school prior to a head injury, so there may not be much difference in their school activities. The answers you'll want to look for while tracking are therefore: Is there a noticeable change? Are they now doing worse? Are they trying just as hard, if not harder, and seeing poorer results? How long has this been going on?

For an athlete of any age, you should consider a baseline test. Typically, such a test is given prior to the start of the athletic season. Measuring attention, visual memory, reaction time, coordination, and testing eyesight, hearing, etc., prior to participation in sports provides baseline information. Should an athlete later have a possible concussion or head injury, you can then compare the pre- and post-concussion test scores. This will provide an idea of which, if any, brain functions or motor skills may be affected.

Parents should look into baseline testing prior to participation by their son or daughter in sports such as football, lacrosse, hockey, soccer, basketball, cheerleading, gymnastics or martial arts, among others. Once tests are completed, which is typically in less than an hour, the results should be saved by the doctor, or medical facility, as well as the parents. Since children continue to grow, and their baseline levels will change as they develop, it is advisable to do a new baseline test every year or two. This way, you are not comparing the post-concussion levels of a 15-year old to the baseline test results of a 12-year old.

Baseline tests can play a very significant role in the recovery from a concussion. You are able to measure how close the concussion sufferer is to his or her baseline results over a period of time. Since people recover from concussions at varying rates, baseline testing can provide an indicator of how far along the patient is on the road to recovery.

Baseline testing is recommended by both the National Collegiate Athletic Association (NCAA) and the American Academy of Pediatrics (AAP).

PACE (Protecting Athletes through Concussion Education) is the nation's largest baseline concussion screening initiative. DICK's Sporting Goods Foundation and partners at ImPACT® are working to build awareness and information so that every athlete, every team, and every school can be smart about concussions.

According to a 2011 study conducted by the University of Pennsylvania School of Medicine, a sideline test has also been able to accurately detect athlete concussions in minutes. In general, sideline testing has not been found particularly accurate at assessing whether or not an athlete has a concussion when he or she comes off the field. However, the test, called the King-Devick Test, captures impairments of eye movement, attention, language, and other symptoms of impaired brain function. The King-Devick Test is an objective remove-from-play sideline concussion screening test that coaches or parents can easily administer in a couple of minutes. It displays a series of single digits on cards or on an I-pad. If the athlete has had baseline testing and takes longer to complete the test after a head injury, he or she should be removed from play. Learn more at kingdevicktest.com.

Doctors and medical professionals continue to explore various means of sideline testing in hopes of finding better ways of diagnosing a possible concussion or brain injury as quickly as possible.

CHAPTER 9

Increased Likelihood of a Second Concussion

S tudies and reports generally agree that youths who have had a concussion are at higher risk for subsequent ones. In fact, it is suggested by researchers that a youngster who has had one concussion may be twice as likely to have a second one as a child/teen who has never had a concussion. A youngster/teen who has had two concussions may be two, three, or even four times as likely to have a third one. The likelihood of subsequent concussions increases with each one. According to Dr. John DiFiori, Chief of the Division of Sports Medicine at UCLA's Geffen School of Medicine, data now suggests that athletes who have three or more concussions are five times as likely as other people to have mild cognitive impairment.

A study in the fall of 2013 from Boston Children's Hospital illustrated that children and teens also take longer to recover from a concussion if they have had one previously. For the study, a concussion was defined to include any altered mental status within four hours of injury and headache, nausea, vomiting, dizziness, and/or balance problems, fatigue, drowsiness, blurred vision, memory difficulty, or trouble concentrating.

The study confirmed what has been believed by the medical community, that the second concussion is more dangerous than the first one. This means that parents, doctors, and coaches need to be that much more conservative following a second concussion.

The long-term effects of multiple concussions are currently being studied by researchers around the globe. Many retired athletes, including former Pittsburgh

Steelers' star Terry Bradshaw, can attest to such long-term effects. After more than half a dozen concussions, the famed quarterback began noticing a slowing of short term memory along with impairment in his hand-eye coordination during his years as a sports commentator and analyst. While Bradshaw is being treated, it is not anticipated that he will recover; but the hope is to minimize the progression of symptoms.

Not only can multiple traumatic incidents contribute to the development of mild cognitive impairments (MCI's), but multiple concussions can lead to post-concussion syndrome (PCS), discussed earlier, and chronic traumatic encephalopathy (CTE), which is a progressive degenerative disease of the brain found in athletes (and others) from repetitive brain trauma, including symptomatic concussions as well as asymptomatic subconcussive hits to the head. This head trauma triggers progressive degeneration of the brain tissue, including the build-up of an abnormal protein called tau.

Such changes in the brain can occur months or even years after the brain trauma, as being evidenced by former NFL and NHL players as well as boxers. CTE symptoms include memory loss, confusion, impaired judgment, impulse control problems, aggression, depression, and, eventually, progressive dementia. Following the suicide of former NFL defensive star Junior Seau, it was reported that he had been suffering from CTE. Clearly, recovering from each concussion is a greater challenge but is also that much more significant. Failing to do so adequately can lead to additional neurologic damage.

Some Concussion Statistics

There are numerous statistics floating around out there regarding the increase of concussions in youth sports. The Center for Disease Control (CDC) provides a number of statistics that parents, coaches, and young athletes should be aware of – as a cautionary tale. They have also started the *Heads Up* initiative to provide important information on preventing, recognizing, and responding to a concussion. For more, you can visit the *Heads Up* website at www.cdc.gov/concussion/HeadsUp/.

Among the statistics you will find from the CDC and elsewhere are:

- It is estimated that somewhere between five and ten percent of all athletes will get a concussion in a given sports season. Football has the highest probability with a 75% chance of concussions for males, and soccer has a similarly high 50% chance of a concussion for female athletes.
- The majority of sports-related concussions, 78%, occur during games rather than training or practice.
- The most common symptoms are headaches and dizziness (70%+), while fewer than ten percent of players who get a concussion lose consciousness (this also dispels the myth that loss of consciousness is very common in concussions).
- While football is known for hard hits, with an estimated 25 MPH speed of a player hitting a stationary player, many parents, coaches, and athletes underestimate the potential for concussions in soccer, despite the literature to the contrary. Consider that, according to the CDC, the impact speed of a soccer ball being headed by a player is 70 MPH.

Troubled Teens with TBI

A 2011 Ontario Student Drug Use and Health Survey of more than 4,500 students illustrated that teens who reported having lifetime traumatic brain injuries had a 52% higher risk, or increased levels, of psychological stress as compared with peers who had not had such injuries. Poor conduct in school, bullying, depression, and even suicidal thoughts were found to be more common among students with TBI.

CHAPTER 10

Minimizing the Risk and Teaching the Fundamentals

There is no surefire way to prevent concussions in sports. There are, however, ways to minimize the risk. First and foremost, protective gear should always be worn in contact sports including (but not limited to) football, hockey, lacrosse, wrestling, and hockey as well as in other sports including baseball and activities such as martial arts.

But it's not just about "wearing" protective gear. Coaches should make sure that each player is wearing the proper gear. Too often, players borrow gear that is too big for them, doesn't fit quite right, or they wear broken helmets with cracks or no chin strap. If the gear is faulty, it loses much of its protective capacity. Head gear should fit properly and not move around. The wrong head gear increases the risk of head injuries.

Risks are also minimized if leagues play using age-appropriate rules. Yes, there are tackle football leagues for kids as young as six or seven. With all due respect, there are also beauty pageants for three year olds and child labor in many countries. The point? Tackle football is not something children of six or seven years of age should be playing. Despite the popularity of Pop Warner football leagues, the majority of coaches, parents, and doctors today are starting to agree that youngsters are too susceptible to serious injuries at those ages. Consider that even Tom Brady did not strap on the pads until he was a freshman in high school – and it didn't exactly slow down his career.

The age at which youngsters begin playing contact sports is up to the parents. BUT when it comes to children under ten playing tackle football, it is very often more for dads then it is for the youngster. It is not usually about responsible parenting or coaching. A perfect example comes from a game played in Mississippi in late 2011. It was a 52 point onslaught between two very mismatched teams of ten year olds and was recounted in the news because five boys (all age ten) left with head injuries. Neither coach had sense enough to stop the game...both were suspended.

There are so many problems with youngsters playing contact sports at very young ages that it's hard to know where to begin. Besides the obvious injury risk is the problem that coaches, in most cases, are simply volunteers who can put the lineups and the plays together but have no idea what to do if a kid gets hurt. Many such coaches even acknowledge that they are fearful of such a scenario and pray it doesn't happen to one of the kids they are coaching. There are also vast size differences in youngsters' growth as well as in their skill levels and their understanding of how to play the sport correctly. Gross mismatches can exist and can lead to serious injuries.

A study reported in the *Journal of Neurology & Neurophysiology,* conducted over an 11-year time span from January of 2000 through December of 2012, focused on young athletes (ages 5-13) playing football and was reported by those evaluated in Emergency Departments. They recorded 2,028 concussions (average 184.4 per year) as captured by the National Electronic Injury Surveillance System (NEISS) database of the U.S. Consumer Product Safety Commission. Based on the national number of athletes in this age range, the total number (using the same averages) would be 49,185 concussions (avg. 4,471 per year), and these were only the ones that were brought into emergency rooms. We already know that it is likely that at least 50% of concussions do not result in visits to doctors, and this does not include those that visited their personal or family doctors. The mean age of the study was 11.2 years of age.

The study concluded with: *Clinical Relevance: Younger children are more susceptible to long-term [effects] from head injuries and, thus, improved monitoring systems for these athletes are needed to assist in monitoring patterns of injury, identifying risk factors, and driving the development of evidence-based prevention programs.*

Teaching the Fundamentals

There are fundamentally sound ways to learn, play, and enjoy sports; many include ways that minimize contact until kids know how to play a contact sport properly and are more developed physically.

To learn football, for example, flag football provides all of the skills except tackling. As for baseball, after T-ball, having coaches pitch is also advised for young children. Besides not having to watch a game with 200 walks (in which the kids are bored to tears), children are less likely to get hit in the head by a pitcher damaging his or her arm while trying to throw an occasional strike.

Parents are catching on. Reports show that Pop Warner football, the nation's largest youth tackle football program, has seen a ten percent drop in the past four years, with more kids opting for flag football – or at least their parents making the decision for them.

One sports franchise league, i9 Sports® based in Tampa, Florida, is the nation's first and largest provider of youth sports leagues in the United States with over 600,000 members spanning 500 communities from New York to Hawaii. They have seen an impressive 18% growth rate in flag football in recent years. They explain that local families are leaving tackle football because of head injury and concussion fears and are joining flag football as a safer alternative. It's also noteworthy to mention that many current and former NFL players choose flag football over tackle for their own children. They learn the fundamentals of the game before having to deal with the hard hits.

Many young soccer leagues are also now thinking about the idea of banning heading for youngsters until their neck muscles are strong enough to withstand the impact of a ball coming from 50 yards away. Again, this is a way of minimizing the growing number of head injuries and concussions in a sport that can still be great fun at any age.

It is somewhat ironic how many parents will talk about not teaching a youngster to throw a curve ball at a young age for fear he or she will damage his/her arm. Yet, those same parents will be fine with their child making a tackle, correctly or incorrectly. Shouldn't they worry about kids damaging their brains? Are we really still a nation of brawn over brains?

It's also important to make sure that any activity is realistically suited for your child's age and physical capabilities. Not everyone will be the right match for every sport. Parents need to know when they are pushing a child into a sport that he or she is either not interested in playing or is not physically capable of playing at a given age, or ever. Be realistic.

CHAPTER 11

Addressing Concussion Symptoms

Yes, there is a wealth of material written about concussions and head injuries these days, particularly in regard to sports. The lawsuits by former NFL and NHL players have drawn a lot of media coverage, and rule changes at the professional level will hopefully trickle down through the all–important school sports programs and even non-school competitive leagues.

But what happens if and when the damage is ongoing? What happens to those who have already had concussions or head injuries? How do they change the course of life to make it more productive? What happens when, despite the best intentions, an athlete takes a blow to the head next week, next month, or next year and does not recover in the three to five weeks anticipated by his or her doctor?

While there are so many articles about detecting a concussion or head injury and keeping an eye on the symptoms to see that they go away in a reasonable amount of time, the question remains, what happens for the percentage of people who continue suffering? What happens to the young girls who loved playing soccer, mentioned earlier in the book? For the athletes who are now feeling the effects of blows to the head 10, 15, or 20 years ago like Terry Bradshaw, among many others?

It is with this in mind that I want you to keep on reading. Providing you with information about concussions is important as is talking to – and listening to – your child. My goal, however, as mentioned earlier, is to provide something more, a solution when symptoms do not go away. You cannot find this information in any of the articles or books you may find. You'll learn all about concussions; but when it comes down to doing something about the long-term effects, they usually say, "You'll need to seek out additional help." The Irlen Method provides such help. It can alleviate most, if not all, of the symptoms that have been mentioned resulting from a concussion. With that in mind, I want to discuss what I've been doing for more than three decades and how such work has helped many children and adults with the persistent symptoms that have continued after a concussion or brain injury.

CHAPTER 12

Irlen Spectral Filters: A Solution

What are Irlen Spectral Filters? How can they help?

In the upcoming sections, I want to answer those questions with some assistance from a number of people whose quality of life has been vastly improved after head injuries thanks to Irlen Spectral Filters.

I will re-state upfront, and emphatically, that Irlen Spectral Filters are not a magical cure but have eliminated many of the symptoms and problems resulting from a head injury, concussion, and whiplash for thousands of children and adults so that life is no longer a struggle and allowed them to return to a productive and meaningful life which best resembled what life was like prior to their head injuries.

A Brief History

It seems like a lifetime ago, in the 1970s, that while working as a school psychologist in Southern California, I encountered numerous children of all ages with reading problems and a similar number of parents concerned and frustrated as to why their children continued to struggle with reading year after year. It became evident that not all children would simply outgrow reading problems or improve with instruction and remediation.

Fast forward to the 1980s when, as Director of the Learning Disability Program at a local university, I was conducting research with a group of university students who struggled academically because of reading difficulties, even though they had good reading skills. I became interested in studying adults, rather than youngsters, because adults give more reliable reports, have greater insight, and have had years of remediation and other interventions. They would provide me with an opportunity to ask new questions in order to determine problems that may have stayed with an individual for a lifetime without ever being identified or addressed. It was while working with these adults that I began to ask questions that, much to my surprise, led to new information. Many of them told me that, after reading for a while, words no longer stayed still on the page or were easy to see. I never expected that words and letters moving about the page was the problem, but there it was, explained by several people. Even more surprising was the reporting that reading created physical symptoms. Could these problems be addressed by methods already in existence? I thought that it was certainly possible and asked the adult students to be examined by experts, which they agreed to do. They were seen by optometrists, developmental optometrists, ophthalmologists, neurologists, psychologists, and reading specialists. Many recommendations were implemented, but nothing changed. It became clear that I needed to create a method to solve the problems that these students were reporting.

Of significance was the discovery that reading actually triggered physical symptoms for some people. Reading tests and psychoeducational tests never address or even ask about physical symptoms. On one hand, if you've never experienced these problems, why would you think that it would be different for others? On the other hand, if you always fall asleep while reading, you assume that the purpose of books is to put you to sleep. Or if you get headaches when reading, you assume that everyone gets a headache if they just read long enough. Obviously, the majority of the population assumes that everyone is like them and can read for hours without any discomfort. It must be mentioned that in time we found that the Irlen Method eliminated these physical symptoms so that individuals were able to read and do other academic tasks for longer time periods because it was comfortable and the print remained easy to see. This is an important point to remember when we talk about the effects of concussions.

Jumping ahead in the story one more time, by testing, doing research, and reviewing again and again what these adult students were explaining, it became clear that this was a type of visual processing deficit and not a vision problem. Visual processing involves the brain's ability to accurately understand and process visual information. Academic and work performance, behavior, attention, ability to sit still, and concentration are some of the areas that can be affected when visual information is not processed properly by the brain.

In essence, the eyes act as the camera which directs the information to the correct part of the retina; however, it is the brain that processes and interprets the information. It is not uncommon for the brain to translate items differently than they appear. For example, if you look at an optical illusion, you will see how the pictures can appear to move or change in front of you, while they are actually not moving at all. When you watch a 3-D movie, your eyesight isn't changing, but your brain is processing it in a different way through 3-D glasses. This was the foundation for discovering what was initially called Scotopic Sensitivity Syndrome, which later came to be known as Irlen Syndrome. It is a visual processing disorder that is often inherited but may be caused by other factors such as concussions, whiplash, or head injury.

Without getting into the details, we became aware that the problem was in the connection from the eyes, through the visual pathways and into the brain. Through months and months of experimentation, it was color that emerged as the method for providing stability and clarity. Again, using 3-D glasses as a comparison, the brain reacts to the 3-D images through the special filters to make things appear closer to you than they really are. If you take the glasses off, the entire experience is completely different and what you are looking at on the screen is blurry. I use this simple comparison just to show how the brain and colors can function as a way to change perception.

It All Began with Colored Overlays

I discovered that colors used as overlays or plastic sheets placed over the page of printed material could change the way it appeared to the individual. BUT, the same color did not work for everyone. In fact, numerous colors or even color combinations were needed as different people, or should I say people's brains, needed different colors.

My initial breakthrough actually began discovering that color allowed adults and children to read better than ever before – they were more comfortable and read faster, longer, and with flow, fluency, and good comprehension.

But these students wanted more. Sure, they could read with comprehension and see numbers easily on a sheet of paper, but what about reading on computer screens, iPads, iPhones, and copying from whiteboards? The students asked me to make everything they looked at in their environment better.

It was a tall order; but, of course, I wanted to help them. So I decided to try the same colors that they used as overlays but instead as lenses. The colors which helped as overlays didn't work as lenses, so we needed to find different color combinations that would work in all situations. It took time, but it worked. In the end, the colors worn successfully as glasses turned out to be different from their colored overlays. In addition, each person needed their own specific color, or combination of colors, for the glasses. Wearing colored lenses, which I called Irlen Spectral Filters, turned out to be even better than overlays as they made so many more activities easier and more comfortable, while working for reading as well. Colored filters clearly made a huge difference!

In some instances, the lenses were a combination of as many as five, six, or more different colors combined into one set of lenses to create the glasses. It is a very technical process because of the multitude of possible colors, and variations in densities are unique for each person as each individual's brain is uniquely different. Remember, one shoe size does not fit everyone. Eventually, I created a method of testing to determine the colors and finally started providing filtered glasses to a group of adults. With these new lenses, the adult students were excitedly reporting the improvement in their perception and abilities, including academic, depth perception, and, equally important, the elimination of physical symptoms including headaches, fatigue, dizziness, eye pain, and eye strain.

Of course, as this was happening, word was also spreading; and people were coming in seeking testing for the "magical" colored filters. However, before expanding the technology, it was important to make sure that the changes were not temporary. As the adult students themselves said, "Don't change things and make them better unless it can stay this way and not go back to the way it was before." So we watched and waited, getting reports from those who were wearing their Irlen Spectral Filters. A month, three months, six months, a year...the filters were still helping! They did not stop working! And everyone wearing their Irlen Spectral Filters reported that they could clearly see the difference.

CHAPTER 13

Good News Travels Fast

t was halfway around the world, in the land down under, that the story of my discovery first hit the air waves, thanks to an Australian journalist who came with his daughter to the United States looking for a solution to his daughter's reading difficulties. The Australian version of *60 Minutes* aired the story, and the response was tremendous - the largest response in the history of the program, resulting in an influx of calls and letters. Before I knew it, I was off to Australia to train professionals in the Irlen Method and to do interviews for a very receptive audience. Soon, New Zealand and Great Britain would follow with major news stories that also resulted in a public demand for local clinics. Then in 1988, the USA version of *60 Minutes* aired their own story about the Irlen Method, "Reading by the Colors," which drew an avalanche of phone calls and letters, overwhelming the phone lines, and even shutting down the phone lines to California from people identifying themselves as having this problem and desperate to get help for themselves and their children.

Pretty soon, I found myself training professionals in the USA and all around the world. In a short time, tens of thousands of children and adults had been helped by wearing Irlen Spectral Filters and millions of children and adults were using colored overlays.

Newspaper articles followed, many as a result of people telling their stories to reporters and local media outlets and posting blogs, such as the ones below. They wanted to share their good fortune with others, becoming very strong advocates.

We also received letters, and some folks started posting their Irlen stories on the Internet.

Here is my daughter and her daddy with their lenses! They have been life changing. We love Irlen filters! I currently work as a Special Ed teacher and will be getting trained as an Irlen Screener!!! **Aliscia Ferlito-KreciszKids**

———⌾———

I'm so proud of my lil' lady Chloe. This is what she came home from school with today. She has come so far and made so much progress since getting her 'magic' glasses...she has her SATS next week and says she is actually feeling ok about doing them now instead of being scared. Bless her. **Jenny Robinson**

———⌾———

My son, Oscar, is very thankful for his new lenses. Irlen lenses don't just change lives, they save lives. Thank you. **Robin May**

———⌾———

I was told by my English teacher to write a poem about something close to my heart, so I wrote this :

I sit in class
The paper glares
Rivers appear and words move

Penny G.

———⌾———

So many children fall thru the cracks. My son was diagnosed at 23 yrs old. Apparently, schools know about this syndrome, yet fail to pass it along to parents as a possibility

of the reason the child is doing poorly in school. I really wish someone told me about it years ago.
Deb Ganney

The change is so dramatic that many people simply do not believe it. Having seen this over and over, I so wish all students having challenges in reading would be screened.
Patricia L. Wenzel

Irlen Filters Rock My World. My daughter was having difficulty completing her school work. Her teacher convinced us that she was doing it on purpose to avoid doing her homework. As it turned out, she was not. It is not an understatement to say her life is better today. She is able to do school work faster and without complaining; she is not constantly rundown, fidgety, complaining of headaches and stomachaches, and being tired. She has discovered the joy of reading for pleasure. She now absolutely loves math. She is a happier, more confident child. She had some learning to catch up on; but by the 6th grade, her grades had gone from just passing to mostly 10's with a few 9's. As a parent, it is just wonderful to see her excel and to enjoy learning. I am grateful that I discovered Irlen Filters for her. **Jennifer J.**

Naomi was not diagnosed with Irlen Syndrome until she was in the 4ᵗʰ grade. However, since first grade, she had complained about having headaches, not being able to see the board, saying her eyes hurt, and coming home not only tired, but complaining of stomachaches and headaches. She had regular eye exams and physicals. Each doctor always gave her a clean bill of health, so we basically let her comments slide.

After having her tested for Irlen, I wanted to cry. During the testing, it was evident that she could only see one letter at a time. It is no wonder she was not reading well. Math was also a problem. She would jump up and down and scream that she couldn't do it and that she hated math. Again, if you can only see one number at a time, there is no way to do math. Watching her being tested for the filters was amazing.

During the Irlen testing, she was asked to copy a sentence. It took her several minutes and considerable effort because she had to look at each letter. With her Irlen Filters, when given a new sentence to copy, she not only quickly copied it down, but she did not have to use her finger to go back and forth from letter to letter. She could just look over and copy a few words at a time. **Carrie G.**

People were writing articles and posting blogs about their experiences, such as this one by Christina England: Is Your Child Really Dyslexic or Do They Suffer from Irlen Syndrome?

You can check out her blog at: www.missecoglam.com/health/item/6951-is-your-child-really-dyslexic-or-do-they-suffer-from-irlen-syndrome?

CHAPTER 14

So, What Does All This Have to do With Concussions and Head Injuries?

G ood question, one that opened my eyes to new possibilities for helping a population that had acquired Irlen-like symptoms. It was a woman named Lu with a serious head injury who first contacted me back in 1998, after looking at the Irlen website and reading stories like those above. She was experiencing the same type of reading problems, physical symptoms, and other difficulties as the struggling readers by her symptoms following a head injury in 1991, as a result of a car accident. In addition to reading difficulties, she was struggling with headaches and migraines, seizures, extreme light sensitivity, depth perception problems, poor motor coordination, disorganization, and disorientation. She had great difficulty pulling her thoughts together, and communicating with others had become near impossible.

After her head injury, Lu had been seen by neurologists as well as psychiatrists and various other doctors. She had MRI's and CAT scans and years of various therapies. However, she found no relief or solutions for her symptoms, so she isolated herself at home. Even at home, while trying to do simple everyday tasks, she would find herself extremely exhausted and spent most of her time lying down. When she first came to the Irlen Institute, she needed to use a walker as her balance and coordination were problems. Her life had been like this for seven years.

Not unlike many individuals who have sustained concussions or more serious head injuries, Lu was so traumatized and overwhelmed by the change in her ability to function that she had only focused on a few of her symptoms. It is not unusual for people to miss the correlations between their head injury and what can be a number of symptoms. People do not realize that the brain controls how we think, feel, act, perform, and function.

Lu had so many symptoms beyond reading that I was not sure that we would be able to address all of her symptoms. I asked her to please keep a diary tracking her changes and how rapidly the changes occurred wearing her Irlen Spectral Filters. Before she left the office that very first day, she was given her lenses and there was an immediate change. Her headache had subsided and some of her other symptoms also seemed to disappear almost immediately. However, it was very important to know whether or not these changes would continue over time.

Three months later, Lu returned, entering the Irlen Institute without her walker. That was the first good sign. She hugged me and sat down to review her notes. I didn't know what to expect, but thus far it was looking promising. As Lu ran through the list of symptoms that she had been struggling with for seven years, she started to cry. Sure enough, almost every symptom was either gone or significantly better. The Irlen Spectral Filters had done more than I had anticipated. Lu explained that the difference was so profound that she put her Irlen Spectral Filters on before she opened her eyes in the morning and took them off after closing her eyes at night. She was even known to forget she had them on and wear them in the shower.

I asked her if we could video tape her with her Irlen Filters. She was fine with the idea and easily able to handle motor tasks with her filters. Her headaches and dizziness were nonexistent. However, it was when I asked her to take her Irlen Filters off that she became a little apprehensive. I reassured her that she did not have to do this if she did not want to; but in the safety of our offices, she agreed to do so and took off her filters. Within minutes, she was unable to carry on a conversation, pick up a glass, or strike the numbers on a calculator, all of which she could do without any difficulty wearing her Irlen Spectral Filters. Her headache and other physical symptoms took over, and she felt too sick to continue. She broke down and cried, realizing that this had been her life for the past seven years. It had taken only minutes for all her symptoms to return without her Irlen Spectral Filters. Clearly, they had made a huge difference in her life. We immediately encouraged her to put them back on, which she did.

Her changes were so dramatic that she soon started an online support group to share her experience with others. As she states on her website: *I was really injured from a blunt force trauma that drastically changed my life, desire, goals, and lifestyle; and with my Irlen Spectral Filters, my life has changed to a brighter, active, and productive future. They have saved my life. Before my Irlen Filters, my brain was in a perfect storm. When I put on my Irlen Filters, things calmed down. It feels like a message. I can breathe, think clearer, process, and understand things. Any cause, such as a stroke, diabetes, brain injury, blunt force trauma, concussion or whiplash, can cause light sensitivity which results in reading and speech difficulties, memory loss, and poor balance and coordination. You can empower yourself with the knowledge that there may be a solution...Irlen Spectral Filters.*

Fortunately, word spread slowly at first, giving me time to develop new screening and testing methods to help this new population with head injuries with more severe symptoms. New questionnaires were created and self-tests were added, one of which evolved over the years into the self-test featured later in this book.

A Whole New World

To borrow a phrase from Disney, we were soon working with a whole new world of clients, if you will. From concussions to TBI to whiplash, a new population was contacting the Irlen Institute in California and Irlen Centers in the U.S. and worldwide.

Doing follow-up evaluations has always been an important part of the Irlen Method, and it was equally important to continue to document the areas of improvement of those with head injuries as with those who came to seek help for reading problems. Clearly, the Irlen Spectral Filters were making life significantly better for people with head injuries, concussions, and whiplash by alleviating or eliminating many of their symptoms.

CHAPTER 15

In Came the Athletes

Mark had sustained 12 concussions playing ice hockey in high school. He sustained an additional four concussions engaged in martial arts training while in the military. Mark knew it was time to address his symptoms before they made life even more difficult than it had already become.

During the initial interview, I asked whether he had played sports in high school and experienced any concussions, to which he replied, "Ice hockey and lots of concussions. We all did." My next question was what type of student was he in high school, and he replied, "I was not a very good student. I wasn't interested in school." I asked if he always had difficulty in school. It was not until we discussed his academic life that he realized that he had been a good student and suddenly made the connection between his grades dropping significantly during high school and the many concussions he had received while playing ice hockey. Changes in academic performance are frequently overlooked or attributed to other reasons.

According to Mark, his most significant symptoms were light sensitivity, headaches which often became migraines, and feeling nauseous along with his migraines, especially when he was reading and under fluorescent lighting. He never mentioned his headaches and migraines, not in high school or in the military. No one asked him if he had headaches, and he forgot that they were not a part of his life before his concussions. This is also not uncommon. People begin to adjust to their symptoms and accept them as normal. It's like wearing shoes that are too small and, after a while, getting used to feeling uncomfortable. The pain doesn't go away. You simply forget what it is like to walk pain-free.

After our initial interview, Mark met with an Irlen diagnostician who had a briefcase full of different colored lenses. One by one, she would pull out lenses and Mark would look through them. It is a precise process to determine the exact colors that the brain cannot process accurately and filter just those colors. The art of the Irlen process is that each individual needs his/her own unique color, or color combination, which enables the brain to process visual information normally without any stress. Once Mark had his unique combination of colors, the change was instant. "It was amazing that the combination of colors immediately eliminated my headaches inside and outside, and I could read easily and without pain," says Mark.

Sports injuries and concussions, in particular, are not new. They have been brought to the forefront of media because of their increasing occurrences and because the previous generation of professional athletes, football and hockey players in particular, have successfully sued organizations such as the NFL and the NHL.

Nick Bell was one of the professional athletes to appear at our door. He had played in the NFL in the early 1990s. As a running back, he took his fair share of hard hits as running backs typically do. Physical injuries and the wear and tear of the game forced Bell from the field to coaching for a semi-pro football team and eventually to an IT position, which he enjoyed for several years. But Bell soon found that he was struggling with headaches, light sensitivity, and other problems not uncommon to many ex-NFL players; and, rather than going away over time, they were getting worse.

When we saw Nick Bell, he had not just come off the field days or weeks earlier. He was now in his 40's and had not played football in nearly 20 years. His life had rapidly started to decline, something that is also not unusual with ex-football players or ice hockey players. The light sensitivity, headaches, and inability to handle many tasks had forced him to retire from his job at the early age of 40.

"I felt like my brain was tired, and I was in pain most of the time," explained Bell. Willing to take a chance on the possibilities of making some improvements in his life, Bell came to the Irlen Institute. "I didn't know what to expect when I went there," says Bell.

After several months of wearing the color combination that "worked" for Bell, he wrote:

Dear Helen,

I feel compelled to let you know how you and your kind staff have assisted me and my family by working with me on the multitude of medical issues that I exhibit. I cannot begin to explain how the Irlen Institute has profoundly changed my life.

As a professional football player, I experienced 25 - 30 impacts to the head per game while performing as a running back at all levels, from high school to the pros.

I suffered repeated concussions, some reported but most not, because of the fear of losing my job which supported my family. Nevertheless, I suffered from a multitude of physical and psychological issues as a result of playing professional football. It should be noted that when I left college and was drafted by a team, I had "NO" significant issues to my physical or mental well-being.

It has been difficult to receive the appropriate care necessary to attempt to maintain any semblance of a normal life. I suffered with intermittent bouts of depression, varying degrees of anxiety and paranoia, continuous headaches, with extreme light sensitivity, spontaneous loss of balance, motion sickness and continuous severe tinnitus, better known as ringing in my ears, just to name a few.

My psychiatrist, Dr. Daniel Amen, recommended that I try to get some relief by using special glasses provided by the Irlen Institute, located in Long Beach, California. I was reluctant at first; however, today, I am a true believer. The glasses assist immensely with several of my symptoms. My headaches and feeling nauseous, motion sickness, and light sensitivity were instantaneously_ gone. I now feel more relaxed. The Irlen lenses are soothing, and I feel a sense of calmness. I humbly thank Helen Irlen and her wonderful staff for their excellent service and continuous support over these past couple of years. Moreover, I look forward to continuously working with them in any capacity that may help others in a similar situation to mine.
Humbly and very respectfully, I remain
Very Sincerely,
Nickolas "Nick" Bell

More Athletes Started Showing Up

From young women and men struggling with headaches, migraines, and light sensitivity from concussions while playing soccer to professional hockey players, athletes started showing up wanting us to help them with their symptoms.

The problem is that many individuals who suffer from a concussion are unaware of the changes. Pain becomes the new normal. Often, they chalk it up to "being an athlete" and acknowledging physical activities will take their wear and tear on your body. Ironically, these players spend an inordinate amount of time working on their muscles and on conditioning to avoid many such physical injuries. But what about the brain?

Many people do not realize when they are suffering as a result to injuries to the brain.

One young man who came in to see us was a former high school athlete now coaching. "Growing up, I tried every sport; and in high school I played football, basketball, baseball, and ran track," says Adam, adding that "it was a lot of fun." But it was during his freshman year, while playing football, that he had his first concussion. He then feels that he had at least five other concussions over his high school sports career. Despite the blows to the head, he would not say anything to his coaches or parents because he wanted to continue playing.

Along with his athletic prowess, Adam was a good student and graduated from high school with a GPA of 3.5. He used his listening skills and his participation in class to help achieve good grades and compensate for not reading his textbooks. After graduating from high school, he went to college on a football scholarship; however, he ended up on academic probation by the end of his freshman year. He was unable to keep up with the demands of his classes, especially when it came to reading. It's much more difficult to get through college without doing much reading than it is to navigate through high school. So, he dropped out of college and was diagnosed with anxiety, ADD, depression, and brain damage probably related to the concussions from sports. He started taking medications for these conditions.

No longer a player, Adam started coaching sports; but he soon noticed that he was really struggling on sunny days. His eyes had become increasingly sensitive to light. It got so bad that standing on the sidelines during practice became difficult. Being outdoors in general and inside under fluorescent lights was uncomfortable to the point of making him feel physically sick. Adam also reported that his eyes and his head hurt; and that, along with headaches, he would feel tired, sleepy, anxious, and irritable.

"I looked online for help for my light sensitivity and found the Irlen Institute," explains Adam, who now wears Irlen Spectral Filters. "The light sensitivity and headaches are now gone and that alone made it so much easier for me to do my job and go about my life without struggling," adds Adam, who also felt less anxiety and depression. He appreciates all the changes resulting from wearing his Irlen Spectral Filters and wears them every day. Adam also returned to college and is pleased that he is doing well.

Like Adam, athletes who acquired symptoms as a result of a concussion have the same academic difficulties and physical symptoms that we have been successfully treating by using the Irlen Method for over 30 years. However, there is a difference... the severity of the symptoms. A brain that has been compromised by a concussion or head injury is not able to function properly. The problems can be much more severe and debilitating, but often people forget what life was like prior to the concussion. Many people with concussions and head injuries experience frustration, anger, anxiety, depression, and fatigue as they put in the same effort as before but cannot achieve the same results. They work harder but perform worse and feel worse. It's a vicious cycle.

There may be red flags that things are not quite right after weeks, months, or even years. These can be addressed with Irlen Spectral Filters. For example:

- Is your child wearing sunglasses, possibly even indoors?
- Is he or she spending more time in darker rooms?
- Does he or she appear to be squinting even if it's not sunny outside, or even indoors?
- Has his or her academic performance suddenly declined?
- Is he or she avoiding reading or no longer reads for pleasure?

It's important to be aware of what to look for once a child has had any type of concussion in order to make a fair determination of whether the symptoms have indeed disappeared, or not. This also means asking questions in a caring manner. After all, kids don't like to answer questions if they feel you are giving them the third degree.

While you may not ask all of the questions at once, you want to find out how they are feeling and if they have physical symptoms. Ask questions such as:

- Are you getting tired while you're in school?
- Have you been feeling dizzy or nauseous?
- Do you have frequent or ongoing headaches during the day?
- Do you have frequent or ongoing stomachaches?
- You'll want to ask if they get any of these symptoms when they are in sun light or under bright lights, such as in the mall, to determine if they have light sensitivity.

You'll also want to ask about academics with questions such as:

- Does it feel uncomfortable when you try to read?
- Does your head, or your eyes, or even your stomach bother you when you read?
- Is it hard to concentrate on what you are reading?
- Do you have to re-read for comprehension?

While tracking your child's academic performance, you can see if he or she is:

- Taking longer to complete tasks that they were able to complete in a timelier manner
- Getting poorer grades on tests
- Taking longer to complete homework
- Taking longer to do reading assignments
- Avoiding reading altogether, which is a key sign, especially if he or she was an avid reader in the past

CHAPTER 16

Let's Talk About the Brain

The visual cortex is where we process visual information. It is where we integrate information from our eyes and information from our other senses, allowing us to create a three-dimensional representation of the world. Injury to the visual cortex results in the inability to accurately process what we see. After all, visual pathways alone account for more than 50% of the brain's pathways and, therefore, are commonly affected in concussions.

As a result of a concussion, the brain has been compromised. Individuals experience the same physical symptoms from sun light, bright lights, glare, headlights, and even dim lighting as well as from reading and other visual activities. Typically, people are aware that sun light is an immediate trigger for discomfort and reach for sunglasses. However, the same physical symptoms occur in the other situations; but they are not immediately evident as they build gradually over time.

If your eyes are open, then your brain is being flooded by light. Light is composed of all the colors of the rainbow traveling at different speeds. However, with a concussion, certain colors are traveling at the wrong speed so that the brain is working harder and more inefficiently to process the information. This results in physical symptoms and distortions. With Irlen Spectral Filters, the signal that is sent from the eyes along the neurological pathways to the brain is now balanced, thanks to the selected colors, causing the brain to process the information more efficiently or more accurately. The net result is that the text is clear, words stop moving, and physical symptoms disappear.

Advanced brain-mapping technology shows both anatomical and functional changes in brain activity that corresponds directly with a reduction of symptoms when the correct color is worn as glasses.

According to Daniel Amen, MD, Medical Director of Amen Clinics, "For the past ten years, my clinics have screened all of our patients for Irlen Syndrome. When appropriate, we have made many referrals to Irlen Clinics; and our patients have successfully used the Irlen Filters to alleviate many symptoms, including headaches, learning and reading problems, light sensitivity, and depth perception issues. In performing before and after scans (SPECT scans) with the Irlen Filters as the only intervention, we have seen the brain become significantly more balanced. I have often been amazed at the improvements our patients have experienced. My sense is that the lenses help filter out certain colors of the light spectrum that are irritating to brain circuits."

CHAPTER 17

In Came the Military: Concussions: Invisible Life-Altering Wound

For the past few years, we have been working with the military. Unlike athletes who are getting cheered, these men and women are in harm's way, their lives constantly on the line as they serve their country. Many return from overseas with brain injuries as well as numerous other physical injuries, along with serious mental and emotional difficulties. Sitting and talking with numerous soldiers, I must say that I have the greatest respect and admiration for what they do and have done for us.

As noted in the Washington Post: *In nearly a decade of war in Afghanistan and Iraq, the number of U.S. service members who have suffered traumatic brain injury has soared. These wounds can permanently alter the service members' personalities and forever impact their lives.* http://www.washingtonpost.com/wp-srv/special/metro/traumatic-brain-injury/ - /brain/

According to Christian Davenport, Washington Post Staff Writer (Sunday, October 3, 2010): *Brain injuries are the signature wounds of the wars in Iraq and Afghanistan. The soldiers are routinely exposed to brain-rattling blasts that can send ripples of compressed air hurtling through the atmosphere at 1,600 feet per second. Now, the soldiers are struggling to come to terms with an often-invisible wound. In some cases, even apparently mild brain injuries can leave a soldier disqualified for service or require lifelong care that critics say the Department of Veterans Affairs isn't equipped to handle. Since 2000, traumatic brain injury, or TBI, has been diagnosed in about 180,000 service members, the Pentagon says. But some advocates for patients say hundreds, if not thousands, more have suffered undiagnosed brain injuries. A Rand study in 2008 estimated the total number of service members with TBI to be about 320,000.*

Although their injuries might not be as visible as a severed limb, the exposure to blasts can alter brain chemistry and cause all sorts of problems. Even mild TBI can have serious consequences. "A blast causes a change in how your brain functions," said Vice Adm. Adam M. Robinson Jr., the Navy Surgeon General. "People have been very, very slow to come to that conclusion, but it's true."

Since March, 2011, we have been investigating the use of Irlen Spectral Filters with military personnel experiencing light sensitivity, headaches, migraines, and a host of other symptoms as a result of combat-related head trauma that have not been successfully remediated through other interventions. Such interventions have included: migraine medications, acupuncture, chiropractic treatments, healing touch, yoga, meditation, vestibular therapy, Botox injections, hyperbaric, and Neurofeedback.

How did these wounded warriors hear about the Irlen Method? Like every population that we have been able to help, it is from word of mouth, reading the Irlen website, blogs, and searching the web for answers. The soldiers, not unlike professional athletes, do not report concussions or the symptoms from head injuries. If they are not bleeding to death or have lost limbs, they continue fighting. They go into battle again and again for our country. It would be disloyal to leave their buddies and not serve their country. They are exposed to countless RPGs, IEDs, and rocket blasts causing post-concussive syndrome and traumatic brain injury (TBI).

While we are so proud of what they do, the price they pay very often destroys their future hopes and dreams. These are young men and women with spouses and children. They leave the military with the hope of being able to work and support their families. Unfortunately, they have to deal with the pain from physical injuries, the trauma of PTSD, and memory difficulties from TBI. In addition, the silent secret is that the soldiers we see at the Irlen Institute and Irlen clinics are incapacitated, many with headaches all day, every day, that vary in intensity and become migraines once to twice a day or week. They also experience nausea, dizziness, fatigue, anxiety, irritability, anger, frustration, depression, poor concentration, and many have difficulty thinking and sometimes communicating because of the pain. They are usually taking one to four different medications for their migraines as well as for anxiety, depression, insomnia, and pain from their physical injuries. Their dreams and hopes of returning from war to a normal life and supporting their families are dashed by their inability to function in job situations. Those who try returning to school to study in hopes of a career struggle in classrooms under fluorescent lights, reading from books and whiteboards, iPads, computers and taking tests, all of which became next to impossible. Even taking computer courses at home is very difficult since sitting in front of a computer screen, even for a short time, can trigger headaches and other physical symptoms.

At the time of writing this book, over 240 servicemen and women have been evaluated and provided with precision Irlen Spectral Filters. The following information is from a study conducted with 178 military personnel diagnosed with medically-resistant headaches and migraines and chronic light sensitivity as a result of combat-related brain or head trauma. Each was seen at the Irlen Institute for treatment. A preliminary questionnaire determined the severity and frequency of headaches and migraines experienced and difficulties in 28 areas of functioning.

The individualized prescribed, precision tinted Irlen Spectral Filters were determined and given to each individual to wear in the form of glasses. After approximately 4-12 weeks, a follow-up survey was conducted to assess reduction of light sensitivity, headaches and migraines, and the other areas. (Additional follow-up surveys are being conducted with those who have been wearing the Irlen Spectral Filters for one year.)

The amount and severity of difficulties experienced were reported on a 0 to 5 scale (0 means "no problem" and 5 means "considerable problem"). The results for the 178 soldiers showed that on average:

- Nearly 100% reduction in headaches and migraines
- 78% reduction in weekly/monthly migraine medication use
- 99% reduction in weekly/monthly OTC medication use
- Light sensitivity eliminated
- Dramatic reduction in fatigue, eye strain, dizziness, and nausea
- Reduced anxiety, irritability, agitation, anger, and depression
- Improvement in reading, math computation, paper-pencil tasks, computer use, and job performance

- Better coordination, balance, depth perception, general perception, tracking moving objects, and marksmanship
- Improved sleep; better driving, particularly at night; more enjoyment of TV, movies, and video games

It is exciting to report that Irlen Spectral Filters have been providing dramatic and immediate relief and improvements. These improvements extend beyond headaches and migraines to impact other areas of life and daily functioning that are crucial to both their ability to remain on active duty and to achieve success as civilians after retiring from the military.

We are pleased to report that Irlen Spectral Filters are able to eliminate the pain and discomfort that other interventions were unable to eliminate. They have provided the servicemen and women with stability and clarity, both on the printed page and in the environment, and improved functioning in more than 26 areas. Sunglasses, tinted lenses, transition lenses, medications, and alternative therapies did not reduce or eliminate their chronic headaches and migraines and other symptoms.

I am glad the military came to us. My heart goes out for them. They do such an invaluable job for our country and have sacrificed so much. It's so rewarding to help these dedicated men and women.

The Servicemen and Women Speak for Themselves

The following is just a sample of the letters of appreciation from our U.S. military.

My Irlen Filters are amazing. They are a ray of hope. I never thought I would be able to do what I did before my head injuries as well as I am doing things now with my Irlen Filters. I never thought I would get back to a level of normal. I have been able to get off my anxiety medications, no longer have headaches or migraines, and I have read two novels in the past few weeks. **N.D.**

───◦◦◦◦───

My Irlen Spectral Filters have been one of the best changes as I no longer have headaches or migraines. I had headaches all day, every day, and migraines twice a day for years before my Irlen Spectral Filters. Now, because of my filters, I no longer take my migraine medications

which tore up my stomach, and I no longer have to take 4-6 Excedrin a day. The difference with the filters is like night and day. Living every day in pain became my norm after 4-5 years.
J.O.

———✺———

One year after I got my filters, I was deployed back to Afghanistan; but this time with my Irlen Spectral Filters. I no longer got angry or irritable and handled the stress of the work much, much better. There were also days that I spent 10-12 hours in front of a computer screen with no residual effect of headaches, migraines, or eye pain. It made my deployment a whole lot easier. The thought of losing my Irlen Filters would be frightening. I never want to go back to the way it was. It is awesome! Thank you.
L.A.

———✺———

I feel smarter, clearer, and more energized with my Irlen Filters. I no longer have anxiety and am not confused. I am now driven to finish tasks. I am 90% back to my old self. I don't feel woozy, angry, or fatigued. I am not agitated or depressed. **G.H.**

———✺———

Since 2005, I had no clue why I was so angry, why my head hurt during my time outside, and why my mind would feel that it was going hundreds of miles an hour; and nobody seemed to understand. Yesterday I was introduced to these glasses, and right on the spot I felt my brain at peace. **O.R.**

———✺———

It is an incredible feeling to know that something, other than prescription medication, can help a brain injury heal. This technology is great. I think that many other military who have suffered from one or many TBI-related injuries can benefit from these glasses. My experience with them has been exceptional, and I look forward to a new pain-free life. **D.H.**

———✺———

If I don't wear them, I have an immediate headache. With my Irlen Filters, I can read, use the computer, watch TV, and do any task without my eyes hurting and getting a headache. I can see again. I am happy. I no longer have to lie down because of having a headache. **T.T.**

Conclusion: Why Are We Telling You All of This?

The objective of writing this e-book is about trying to help people who are struggling. Are pacemakers extending life for people with heart problems? Yes. Are people receiving hip replacements? Yes. Are the latest in dental procedures making life much easier and less painful for millions of people? Yes. Has cataract surgery helped millions of people see better? Yes.

The point is we need to do whatever we can to take care of **all parts of our bodies including the brain.**

That's the goal of this e-book, to share information that can help people; in this case, recover from a brain injury and allow them to maximize their potential and enjoy a life pain-free.

Of course, as Lu's story pointed out and the military can attest to, head injuries are certainly attributed to other sources besides sports. However, sports are resulting in youngsters and adults experiencing head trauma and physical injuries every day. You need to protect and take care of your brain. You need to make sure you and your children take precautions to avoid head injuries. But you also need to know that any concussion, head injury, or whiplash should not be ignored. Write down your symptoms and changes. Track these symptoms or changes carefully to make sure they disappear. If they do not, remember what you have learned about Irlen Spectral Filters.

In the End

For over 40 years I have helped children and adults as a school psychologist, therapist, and adult learning disability specialist; however, discovering and developing the Irlen Method has been by far the most rewarding experience of my professional career.

I feel very blessed to be able to improve the lives of so many people, both in the U.S. and worldwide. As one Irlen Filter wearer wrote, *Irlen Filters are life changing. Taking away my Irlen Filters would be like taking away my soul.*

I am often asked if I plan on retiring, but I cannot think of anything I could do that would be more gratifying and bring me greater joy and satisfaction than being able to make a real difference for so many people. And I, along with all my Irlen Screeners and Diagnosticians, have done just that. We will keep on helping to improve the lives, health and well-being, along with performance and ability to function, for those who have inherited Irlen Syndrome as well as the athletes and the many others who have acquired the same symptoms as a result of concussions or head injuries.

Irlen Spectral Filters cannot eliminate or even minimize the pain from physical injuries. Nick Bell still has no feeling in his feet. But he has less anxiety, no more headaches, can ride in a car without feeling sick, and perform tasks more easily than he could prior to getting his Irlen Filters. Life is better, not perfect. For Adam, the Irlen Filters completely eliminated his problems including light sensitivity, academic difficulties, and physical symptoms so he could return to school and forge a career path. Lu was able to get her life back and enjoy her family again after seven years of struggling with a wealth of symptoms after her car accident.

There are so many stories.

For those of you with young athletes, or simply for your own well-being, if you are aware of any symptoms arising from concussions or head injuries that persist, we're hopeful that you will visit our website for more information on Irlen Spectral Filters and to find a certified Irlen Screener or Diagnostician near you.

Remember, Irlen Spectral Filters can minimize or eliminate the symptoms and put you back in the game of life.

Please visit our website at www.irlen.com.

APPENDIX A

Categorizing Post-Concussion Problems

A fter just one concussion, the brain can no longer accurately process and interpret visual information. The following is a categorized listing of the wide range of problems that can result from a concussion and be eliminated or reduced with Irlen Spectral Filters:

- **PHOTOSENSITIVITY.** Glare, fluorescent lights, bright lighting, sunlight, headlights at night, reading, all visual activities, patterns, iPads, iPhones, movies, TV screens, and computer screens are triggers for headaches and migraines.
- **PHYSICAL SYMPTOMS.** Severe physical symptoms such that eyes become watery, hurt, ache, burn, and feel strained and tired; headaches and migraines; and/or feeling dizzy, nauseous, anxious, frustrated, and agitated.
- **PERCEPTION, READING, AND OTHER VISUAL ACTIVITIES.** Perception, which was not a problem before a concussion, can become very difficult because the words are too hard to see and too painful. The individual can now read only with many breaks before having to stop. The reader may lose his/her place, misread words, have trouble tracking from one line to the next, need to make an effort to stay focused on the word being read, become frustrated, be unable to comprehend the material, and be unable to continue.
- **DISTORTIONS.** The individual has difficulty accommodating high contrast, especially black on white background. The background can become very bright and painful to look at. The background competes with the print so that it takes work to focus. Print is not in focus; words can become unstable

and move, making it necessary to squint, blink, or open the eyes wider trying to make out the letters, words, or numbers.

- **ENVIRONMENT.** Perceptual processing difficulties include stability, clarity, ease, and comfort looking at objects in the environment affecting depth perception. The individual needs to work to see details and bring things into focus.
- **CONCENTRATION & ATTENTION.** Distortions and physical symptoms become increasingly worse, and tasks quickly become increasingly more difficult. This affects concentration and attention. Problems are significantly worse in bright lights, sunlight, and fluorescent lights.
- **PERFORMANCE.** Ability to function is severely compromised. Being outside in sunlight, in rooms with fluorescent lights, on the computer, and reading or doing visual activities are immediate triggers for headaches, migraines, and many other physical symptoms that limit performance of a task.

Yes, we were fortunate that Irlen Spectral Filters opened up a whole new world for people struggling with head injuries and concussions. It was someone like Lu who expanded our horizons beyond reading, allowing us to assist so many people, including athletes like Nick Bell and Adam among others, to get significant help with the following symptoms:

Headaches
Migraines
Photosensitivity (sunlight, glare, lighting, fluorescent lights, headlights)
Stress & Strain (visual activities, listening, TV, computers, reading, patterns)
Poor Concentration & Attention (reading, listening, working)
Fatigued/Drained/Loss of Energy

Dizziness	Depth Perception
Anxiety	Clumsiness
Agitation/Irritability	Poor Coordination
Behavioral Control/Anger	Balance Problems
Nervousness/Fidgety	Reading (comprehension, retention)
Depression	Math (computation, accuracy)
Difficulty Thinking	Paper & Pencil Tasks
Memory Problems	Copying
Driving	Computers, iPhones, iPads

Night Driving	Study Skills
Sleepiness in Car	Test Taking
General Perception	Difficulty Sleeping
Completion of Assignments	Difficulty Pulling Thoughts Together
Enhance the Quality of Life	Performance and Ability to Function

APPENDIX B

Self-Test

Below is a self-test you can use or ask your child to help you fill out. It provides a good overview of the symptoms associated with a concussion.

CONCUSSION / HEAD INJURY SELF-TEST FOR IRLEN SYMPTOMS
(WWW.IRLEN.COM)

When filling out this Self-Test, please circle only Yes, No, or ?

PROBLEMS SINCE YOUR TBI/CONCUSSION	Circle Answer & Rate Severity (1 = Low -- 5 = High)

Are you experiencing any of the following physical symptoms?

Headaches	No	?	Yes	1	2	3	4	5
Migraines	No	?	Yes	1	2	3	4	5
Eye strain/pain	No	?	Yes	1	2	3	4	5
Dizziness	No	?	Yes	1	2	3	4	5
Nausea	No	?	Yes	1	2	3	4	5
Stomachaches	No	?	Yes	1	2	3	4	5
Tired/fatigued/drained/loss of energy	No	?	Yes	1	2	3	4	5
Easily agitated or irritable	No	?	Yes	1	2	3	4	5
Feeling anxious	No	?	Yes	1	2	3	4	5
Feeling depressed	No	?	Yes	1	2	3	4	5

Fidgety	No	?	Yes	1 2 3 4 5
Poor concentration	No	?	Yes	1 2 3 4 5
Slowed thinking	No	?	Yes	1 2 3 4 5
Short term memory loss	No	?	Yes	1 2 3 4 5

During which activities do you experience headaches, migraines, eye pain/strain, or other physical symptoms?

Reading	No	?	Yes	1 2 3 4 5
Computer, iPad, iPhone	No	?	Yes	1 2 3 4 5
Math computation or copying	No	?	Yes	1 2 3 4 5
Paper and pencil tasks	No	?	Yes	1 2 3 4 5
Watching TV	No	?	Yes	1 2 3 4 5

Concentration/Attention:

Has concentration/attention gotten worse?	No	?	Yes	1 2 3 4 5
With reading or school work?	No	?	Yes	1 2 3 4 5
Problems staying on task?	No	?	Yes	1 2 3 4 5
Distracted in fluorescent lights?	No	?	Yes	1 2 3 4 5

Photosensitivity Since Your TBI or Concussion:

Have you become sensitive to light?	No	?	Yes	1 2 3 4 5
Are you bothered by sunlight?	No	?	Yes	1 2 3 4 5
Are you bothered by glare?	No	?	Yes	1 2 3 4 5
Are you bothered by fluorescent lights?	No	?	Yes	1 2 3 4 5
Are you bothered by headlights at night?	No	?	Yes	1 2 3 4 5

In Sun Light:

Do your eyes bother you?	No	?	Yes	1 2 3 4 5
Do you get headaches?	No	?	Yes	1 2 3 4 5
Do you get migraines?	No	?	Yes	1 2 3 4 5
Do you feel dizzy or nauseous?	No	?	Yes	1 2 3 4 5
Do you feel tired or sleepy?	No	?	Yes	1 2 3 4 5
Do you feel irritable?	No	?	Yes	1 2 3 4 5

Do you feel anxious?	No ? Yes	1 2 3 4 5
Do you feel fidgety?	No ? Yes	1 2 3 4 5

In Fluorescent Lights:

Do your eyes bother you?	No ? Yes	1 2 3 4 5
Do you get headaches?	No ? Yes	1 2 3 4 5
Do you get migraines?	No ? Yes	1 2 3 4 5
Do you feel dizzy or nauseous?	No ? Yes	1 2 3 4 5
Do you feel tired or sleepy?	No ? Yes	1 2 3 4 5
Do you feel irritable?	No ? Yes	1 2 3 4 5
Do you feel anxious?	No ? Yes	1 2 3 4 5
Do you feel fidgety?	No ? Yes	1 2 3 4 5

Reading Difficulties:

Has reading become more difficult?	No ? Yes	1 2 3 4 5
Do you get a headache/migraine?	No ? Yes	1 2 3 4 5
Do you read less?	No ? Yes	1 2 3 4 5
Does reading become harder the longer you read?	No ? Yes	1 2 3 4 5
Do you avoid reading?	No ? Yes	1 2 3 4 5
Do you skip words or lines?	No ? Yes	1 2 3 4 5
Do you repeat or reread lines? Do you lose your place?	No ? Yes	1 2 3 4 5
Do you need to take frequent breaks when you read?	No ? Yes	1 2 3 4 5
Do you use your finger/marker to help keep your place?	No ? Yes	1 2 3 4 5
Is your comprehension of what you read weak?	No ? Yes	1 2 3 4 5
Do you reread for comprehension?	No ? Yes	1 2 3 4 5

Driving:

As a passenger, do you become drowsy?	No ? Yes	1 2 3 4 5
When driving, do you become drowsy?	No ? Yes	1 2 3 4 5

Are you bothered by glare on the car in
front of you?   No ? Yes   1 2 3 4 5
Are you bothered by headlights or tail lights
at night?   No ? Yes   1 2 3 4 5
Do you have difficulty judging when to turn
in front of oncoming traffic?   No ? Yes   1 2 3 4 5
Are you certain when making lane changes? No ? Yes   1 2 3 4 5

Copying:

Has copying become more difficult?   No ? Yes   1 2 3 4 5
Do you have difficulty copying from books, a
whiteboard, or overhead?   No ? Yes   1 2 3 4 5
Do you lose your place?   No ? Yes   1 2 3 4 5
Are you slow?   No ? Yes   1 2 3 4 5
Do you make a lot of careless errors?   No ? Yes   1 2 3 4 5
Do you blink or squint a lot?   No ? Yes   1 2 3 4 5

Math Computation:

Do you misalign digits in number columns?   No ? Yes   1 2 3 4 5
Do you have difficulty seeing numbers in the
correct column?   No ? Yes   1 2 3 4 5
Do you make sloppy or careless errors?   No ? Yes   1 2 3 4 5
Do you have difficulty seeing signs, symbols,
numbers or decimal points?   No ? Yes   1 2 3 4 5

Count up the total number of points in each section

Score 0 -3: Your performance and ability to function have not been affected in this area.

Score 4-7: Your performance and abilities are not as good as they used to be.

A score of 8 or higher indicates that your ability to function and perform has been significantly affected and there is a good possibility that <u>all of the "Yes" answers can be eliminated</u> with the Irlen Method.

The higher your score, the more you are struggling to perform and compromising your immune system.

APPENDIX C

Military Success Documented

T he following abstract was published in the international, peer-reviewed, scientific journal, *Brain Injury*, shortly after the Tenth World Congress on Brain Injury, held in San Francisco, California, in March of 2014.

Background: Since March 2011, a study has been conducted investigating the use of Irlen Spectral Filters with military personnel experiencing chronic light sensitivity, headaches, and migraines as a result of brain or head trauma that have not been successfully remediated through other interventions, including migraine medications, acupuncture, chiropractic treatments, healing touch, yoga, meditation, vestibular therapy, Botox injections, hyperbaric, and Neurofeedback.

Methods: A sample of 134 military personnel diagnosed with medically-resistant headaches and migraines and chronic light sensitivity, as a result of combat-related brain or head trauma, were seen at the Irlen Institute for treatment. A preliminary questionnaire determined the severity and frequency of headaches and migraines experienced and difficulties related to 28 areas of functioning. The individualized, precision-tinted Irlen Spectral Filter was determined and given to each individual to wear in the form of glasses. After approximately 4-12 weeks, a follow-up survey was conducted to assess the reduction of light sensitivity, headaches and migraines, and a variety of other areas. Amount and severity of difficulties experienced were reported on a 0 to 5 scale (0 means "no problem" and 5 means "considerable problem").

Results: Results confirmed a nearly 100% reduction in headaches and migraines, 98% reduction in light sensitivity, 80% reduction in weekly/monthly migraine medication use, 99% reduction in weekly/monthly OTC medication use, 88-95% reduction in other physical symptoms (eye strain, dizziness, nausea), 93-97% reduction in academic difficulties (reading, math computation, copying, paper-pencil tasks, computer, job performance), 75-98% reduction in physical difficulties (coordination, balance, depth perception, general perception, tracking moving objects, marksmanship), and 54-64% reduction in emotional symptoms not related to PTSD (anxiety, irritability/agitation, anger, depression). Paired samples t-tests confirmed all improvements were significant at $p<.05$.

Conclusions: For individuals who have suffered head trauma resulting in light sensitivity and chronic headaches and migraines that fail to respond to other standard interventions, Irlen Spectral Filters provide dramatic and immediate relief and improvements. These improvements extend beyond headaches and migraines to impact other areas of life and daily functioning that are crucial to both their ability to remain in active duty and to achieve success after retiring from the military. Irlen Spectral Filters are able to eliminate the pain and discomfort that no other intervention or medication has been able to eliminate, provide stability and clarity in the visual field (both on the printed page and in the environment), and improve functioning in more than 26 areas. Sunglasses, tinted lenses, transition lenses, medications, and alternative therapies did not reduce or eliminate their chronic headaches and migraines and other symptoms. Determination of the precise hue and density of the various wavelengths of light must be individually determined in order to eliminate headaches, migraines, and other symptoms and improve ability to function.

APPENDIX D

Recommended Resources

1. Center for Disease Control and Prevention (CDC) - Home - Concussion in Sports m.cdc.gov/head
   To help ensure the health and safety of young athletes, CDC developed the Heads Up: Concussion in Youth Sports Initiative to offer information about brain injuries.

2. Center for Disease Control and Prevention (CDC) - Heads Up Youth Sports - Concussion - Traumatic Brain Injuries
   www.cdc.gov/concussion/HeadsUp/youth.html

3. Concussions in Sports Article: Nationwide Children's.
   www.nationwidechildrens.org/concussions-in-sports
   Read about concussions in youth sports, including the causes, symptoms, treatment, and prevention of head injuries among young athletes.

4. Head Injury and Concussion in Sports
   sportsmedicine.about.com/.../a/Head-Injury-Concussion-Hub.htm

5. Head Injury and Concussion in Sports: Learn how to recognize a concussion or another serious head injury by Elizabeth Quinn.
   sportsmedicine.about.com/od/injuryprevention/a/Head-Injury-Concussion-Hub.htm

6. Head injury in sports - Brain Injury Resource Center
   www.headinjury.com/sports.htm

BOOKS

7. *Change Your Brain, Change Your Life: The Breakthrough Program for Conquering Anxiety, Depression, Obsessiveness, Anger, and Impulsiveness* by Daniel G. Amen

8. *Making a Good Brain Great: The Amen Clinic Program for Achieving and Sustaining Optimal Mental Performance* by Daniel G. Amen

---

I would like to say thank you to Dr. Daniel Amen, Nick Bell, Dr. Andrew Yellen, the military men and women, and clients who provided their personal stories for this book, as well as everyone at the Irlen Institute and my Irlen Diagnosticians and Screeners, who provided the insight and encouragement to write this ebook. It is the struggles of the individuals who have sought my help that reinforce the need to provide information and solutions. A very special recognition to Rich Mintzer without whose help and guidance this book would not have been possible. Helen

Made in the USA
Columbia, SC
28 March 2020